The Crescent in Light of the Cross

D.M. di Francesco

An Excerpt from the Hymn of Light

The Light of the just and joy of the upright is Christ Jesus, our Lord, Begotten of the Father, he manifested himself to us.
He came to rescue us from darkness and to fill us with the radiance of his light.

Day is dawning upon us; the power of darkness is fading away.
From the true Light there arises for us the light which illumines our darkened eyes.

His glory shines upon the world and enlightens the very depths of the abyss.
Death is annihilated, night has vanished, and the gates of Sheol are broken.

Creatures lying in darkness from ancient times are clothed in light.
The dead arise from the dust and sing because they have a Savior.

He brings salvation and grants us life.
He ascends to his Father on high.
He will return in glorious splendor and shed his light on those gazing upon him.

— St. Ephrem the Syrian (c. 306-373 AD), teacher and orator[1]

---

[1] Translation from the original Syriac Aramaic from Maronitefaith.com

Table of Contents

The Crescent in Light of the Cross

Introducing Christianity to Our Muslim Neighbors

Acknowledgements

My sincerest thanks to all those who offered the advice and guidance that made this work possible, especially my family and friends, Bp. Mansour, and Gabriel Salibi — God bless!

Prologue

In today's globalized world, the relationship between Islam and Christianity has become more ostentatious yet ironically less well understood. Drawn to understanding this issue better—and also because of my Lebanese ancestry, I studied Arabic, Islam, and the Middle East in college. However, as I earned my degree in Middle East Studies and learned about Islam, I grew more and more concerned about how Islam views its own origins and its relationship to other faiths. I'd like to share with you what I've learned in the hope of convincing both Muslim and Christian alike—based on historical, Islamic, and Christian sources—that Christ was truly divine and came to invite all souls to eternal life.

Here's the main idea in one paragraph. Even though Islam claims to descend from Judaism and Christianity, it professes that everything that came before it (the Bible) was corrupted or cancelled out by the Quran. History, however, tells a different story—one that supports the authenticity of the Bible and shows that Islam and the Quran were born of political motives. Islam combined elements of Judaism, Christianity, and Arab culture into a Pan-Arab religion that would likely have had appeal to the various Jewish, Christian, and Arab groups conquered by the early Muslims. Interestingly, Muslims share many of their beliefs about Jesus with heretical Christian groups that lived in Arabia for centuries before Islam—a fact that supports the case for orthodox Christianity and further disproves Islam's *raison d'être*. At the same time, Islam's teachings about Jesus and Christianity strongly discourage Muslims from ever truly learning about Christ. The key to introducing them to Jesus is to faithfully answer the question he asked his Apostles: "Who do you say that I am?" (Mt. 16:15). Beyond challenging Islamic beliefs about the identity of Jesus, we have to share with Muslims the Good News that Jesus is Lord and introduce them to his unconditional love.

God's Kingdom is not of this Earth

In a world filled with turmoil and suffering, every human soul longs for peace. Men have attempted to establish peace and order time and time again—through governments, scientific achievement, and cultural expression—but have always fallen short. The monotheistic faiths tell us that true peace can only be found in God. Yet, they differ on what this peace looks like and how it is achieved. Jews believe that God will establish peace on earth with the coming of the Messiah, God's Anointed One, which will bring about the unity of all peoples in worship of the God of Abraham, Isaac, and Jacob. Muslims have sought peace by the establishment of Islamic societies through the centuries, which enjoin submission to God's will and the message of Islam on believers to prepare for the Day of Judgment. Christians, however, say that true peace is not to be found in this world. Rather, it is found in the Kingdom of God, which is built up in this life and fully established in the next, by loving the Lord and entrusting one's entire being to His hands. In contrast to Judaism and Islam, Christianity proclaims that the human heart truly encounters peace in a Kingdom that is not of this world and that no earthly leader can hope to establish. In a world wearied with conflict, politics, and war, Jesus's message of a heavenly kingdom of peace should grab our attention. Our hope is not to be placed in the rulers or things of this world but in God alone.

Who can we say has achieved peace? Has peace come with the re-establishment of the kingdom of Israel? Or was peace manifest through the Islamic caliphates? Christianity seeks peace not in governments or in earthly kingdoms but in every promise and every word that comes from the mouth of God. We as imperfect human beings cannot create the perfection of God on this earth. Thus, from God's promises and words, Christians gain the confidence and faith to know that this world alone will never satisfy us. Rather, as St. Augustine, an early Christian theologian from modern Algeria, says: "Our hearts are restless until they rest in you [O Lord]." Peace will not come from the works of men—from the building of kingdoms or caliphates—but rather from hands of the Lord.

Christians have certainly blended politics, violence, and religion as Jews and Muslims have, but Christianity itself was not born of politics. Church and state have always existed side-by-side—during the period of persecution under the Romans, during the Middle Ages, and even in modern times. Church and state are interwoven but separate, connected but not blended. Nearly eighteen hundred years after the birth of Jesus, the American colonists would establish a country that separated religion and state not to announce the triumph of men over God but to protect the sanctity of religion from the corrupting influences of politics. As Jesus tells us, "Repay to Caesar what belongs to Caesar and to God what belongs to God," (Mt. 22:21). Government is necessary to provide order, but when unduly blended with religion obscures the fact that the end goal of our lives is not power or status or nice possessions, but the Kingdom of Heaven.

Do we not see that politics, built up by imperfect human beings, cannot provide the human heart with the eternal peace we seek? Do we not see the suffering of the Syrian people, ruled by a dictator who kills his own people? Are we blind to the plight of Yemen, whose children do not have enough food to eat? And what are we to make of the leaders in Iran, Saudi Arabia, and Turkey who mix religion and politics to justify wars and retain their power? Yet, such suffering, born of human imperfection, is not only found in the Middle East. Look at the communist and socialist states, regimes that control and restrict religion to declare the supremacy of man over all. Over fifty million people died in the last century to establish a man-made vision of peace. Even in Europe and the Americas, the political sphere has fought and is fighting to dominate religion. Every human heart desires peace, but Christianity is clear: we will not fully discover or truly comprehend the immeasurable peace of God on this earth.

If we accept this truth, then another question presents itself: If we will not fully find peace in this life, how can we begin to establish this Kingdom of Heaven Jesus talks about? Can violence establish peace or must peace be born of peace? In the time of ancient Israel, God commanded the Israelites to wage war against the people who had settled in the land that was to become the kingdom of Israel. Muslims see in Muhammad a parallel story – a commander of believers fighting through raids and battles to establishing a caliphate dedicated to the One True God. Violence can create an earthly peace for a time, but it is not the lasting peace of God's Kingdom.

The answer to this quest, the search for God's eternal peace, lies in the monotheistic faiths' understanding of the Messiah, God's Anointed One. The prophets spoke of the coming of the Messiah:

"Say to the fearful of heart: Be strong, do not fear! Here is your God, He comes with vindication; with divine recompense, He comes to save you. Then the eyes of the blind shall see, and the ears of the deaf be opened; then the lame shall leap like a stag, and the mute tongue sing for joy. For waters will burst forth in the wilderness, and streams in the Arabah." (Is. 35: 4-6).

In its original Jewish context, the Messiah was the one who would unite the tribes of Israel and bring all nations to worship the God of Abraham,

Isaac, and Jacob, ushering in an era of peace in the world. Islam also calls attention to the Messiah. Like Christianity, Islam claims that the Messiah has already come in the person of Jesus. In the Quran, the name of Jesus is mentioned more often than the name of Muhammad. The Jesus of Islamic tradition is a miracle worker and a healer, performing more wonders than any prophet. In the Quran, Jesus is born miraculously of the Virgin Mary and taken up miraculously to heaven, demonstrating his special relationship with God. Yet, Jesus does not establish the long-awaited kingdom of Israel. While the Quran certainly gives special attention to Jesus, it does not present an explanation for this inconsistency. Only Christianity presents an answer to this problem.

According to Christians, if Jesus as Messiah was not king of this world, then he must be king of the world to come, which he referred to as the Kingdom of Heaven or the Kingdom of God. This is the Kingdom of peace that all men seek. Yet, how can a man reconcile the imperfection of mankind to the perfection of God or blot out the offenses of our human race before the Throne of Majesty? Only God-made-man can do this, for human beings can never bridge the abyss of sin between man and God or repay to God what He does not already possess. This is why Christians believe Jesus is the Son of God—not simply a son in the earthly sense, but begotten of the same substance, the same Divinity, as God Himself.

Rather than establish an earthly reign, Jesus taught his disciples to consider their relationship with God and neighbor and in so doing revealed his special relationship with God.

"You shall love the Lord, your God, with all your heart, with all your soul, and with all your mind. This is the greatest and the first commandment. The second is like it: You shall love your neighbor as yourself. The whole law and the prophets depend on these two commandments," (Mt. 22:38-40).

Peace, like love, is relational. It is found within oneself, between men, and between man and God. Jesus taught his disciples that the Kingdom of peace is built up through opening our hearts to God's love and sharing that love with others, by willing their good and desiring their salvation (from Latin meaning, to make whole). Furthermore, it is in the mystery of love that Jesus reveals how he can be both God and man. Love, though one and indivisible, is composed of three parts: the one who loves, the one loved, and the love itself between them. Thus, our Heavenly Father is the one who loves, the Heavenly Son is the one who is loved, and the Holy Spirit is the love between them—one, indivisible, and perfect. To attain peace, we must first begin with love.

Jesus taught his disciples many things about love and demonstrated his Divine love for them through his life, ministry, and death. Instructing his disciples on a pleasant mount one day, Jesus said: "You have heard that it was said, 'You shall love your neighbor and hate your enemy,'" (Mt. 5:43). After all, this was how ancient societies functioned. Danger was constant, and tribes and nations needed to be on their guard. Islam, too, inherited this belief from ancient Arabian society. Yet, Jesus teaches us something radically different from loving those close to us and hating our enemies. He continues:

"But I say to you, love your enemies, and pray for those who persecute you, that you may be children of your heavenly Father, for he makes his sun rise on the bad and the good, and causes rain to fall on the just and the unjust. For if you love those who love you, what recompense will you have? Do not the tax collectors do the same? And if you greet your brothers only, what is unusual about that? Do not the pagans do the same? So be perfect, just as your heavenly Father is perfect," (Mt. 5:44-48).

Though we often fail, Christians must strive to love our enemies, to will their good and to desire their salvation. Preference in our daily interactions must not be given only to other Christians, but to all people, no matter their race, religion, or tongue — only then can there be peace.

There are many people who call this radical act of love weakness or submission, for Christian love will not stop an enemy from attacking or raiding or persecuting others. Jesus provides the answer once more: "You have heard that it was said, 'An eye for an eye and a tooth for a tooth.' But I say to you, offer no resistance to one who is evil. When someone strikes you on [your] right cheek, turn the other one to him as well" (Mt. 5:38-39). And he teaches us: "But seek first the Kingdom of God and his righteousness and all these things will be given you besides," (Mt. 6:33). And again: "Peace I leave with you; my peace I give to you. Not as the world gives do I give it to you. Do not let your hearts be troubled or afraid," (Jn. 14:27). Yes, the Christian will suffer for the love of God, but what is the alternative — to return hate for hate, violence for violence? The Christian does not love out of a place of weakness, for only by God's divine strength can love swallow up the violence of evil and end the human cycle of war, destruction, and sin. This is why Jesus teaches, "The Kingdom of Heaven is like a merchant searching for fine pearls. When he finds a pearl of great price, he goes and sells all that he has and buys it," (Mt. 13:45-46). To build up the Kingdom of Heaven, to experience a sliver of the peace and love of God's Mercy in this life, to love without worrying about receiving something in return, to live fully for others and for God is priceless and cause for great joy. This is the mission of the Church and the invitation of Christ to all people.

The peace and love of God will indeed be made known, in His time and in His way. For God's ways are not our ways, "For as the heavens are higher than the earth, so are my ways higher than your ways, my thoughts higher than your thoughts," (Is. 55:9). We cannot impose our earthly will on God's because otherwise we humanize Him, and turn the Divine King into a worldly king, distant and removed, who hoards his power and demands loyalty at all costs. The Good News that Jesus came to share with us is that God loves us as a father loves his children: "Can a mother forget her infant, be without tenderness for the child of her womb? Even should she forget, I will never forget you," (Is. 49:15). As our Heavenly Father, God promises us communion with Him—the perfect relation of peace and love—as our inheritance in His Kingdom. Jesus tells us: "Come to me, all you who labor and are burdened, and I will give you rest," (Mt. 11:28). And again: "In the world you will have trouble, but take courage, I have conquered the world," (Jn. 16:33). Jesus promises us love, peace, rest, and communion not as an earthly ruler does but as the Prince of Peace and the Son of God, who draws all people into His Father's kingdom, the Kingdom of God.

Islam and Christianity in Ancient Arabia

Islam originated in Arabia in the early 600s A.D., and the word Islam itself is often translated to mean "submission to the will of God." Muslims believe that God sent prophets throughout the ages to teach humanity worship of the one God and submission to God's will. According to Islamic tradition, God first sent prophets to the Jews and Christians, but they forged the messages they received and corrupted the true history of religion. For this reason, Muslims believe God revealed his unchanging words and teachings in the Quran through a final prophet named Muhammad. In the Quran, God makes repeated references to Jewish and Christian figures and claims that they taught his true revelation and were therefore muslims (lower case m)—meaning one who submits to the will of God. The Quran itself is about the size of the New Testament and contains various stories and teachings unique to Islam in addition to references to or variations of some stories found in the Bible.

Among the core beliefs and practices of Islam are what is called the five pillars of Islam: prayer five times a day, almsgiving, pilgrimage to Mecca, fasting during the Islamic month of Ramadan, and the Islamic profession of faith which declares belief in one God and in Muhammad as an authentic prophet. Islam contains two main sects, Sunni and Shi'a, which formed early on in Islamic history over who should succeed Muhammad as leader of the Muslim community. These sects, which generally have a more decentralized authority structure than Christianity, contain a variety of smaller divisions that vary in matters of belief and interpretation of the Quran and the Hadith (the recorded sayings of Muhammad, which are key to Islamic belief).

After sharing his message of a new revelation, Muhammad would go on to conquer much of Arabia, and his followers would continue what has come to be called the Islamic conquest in the West—conquering from Spain to western India. Among Muslims, this period of war is referred to as the "opening" of the world to Islam, and all that came before it is considered the era of ignorance, termed *jahiliyyah* in Arabic. Islam is currently the second largest religion in the world and quickly growing.

As we'll soon discuss in depth, Islam's relationship to Christianity challenges its historical and religious claims. Islamic beliefs about Jesus closely mirror the beliefs of Christian heretical groups that lived in Arabia during the lifetime of Muhammad, demonstrating that he never truly understood Christianity. Some of the beliefs shared between Islam and these heretical Arabian Christian groups include denying Jesus' divinity, rejecting the Crucifixion, and claiming that the Holy Trinity consisted of

God, Mary, and Jesus (similar to a human family). This major hole in the Islamic narrative, centered on the identity of Jesus Christ, opens Islam to a variety of criticisms about its historicity, especially considering that the Biblical histories precede the Quran by hundreds and even thousands of years.

A More Detailed Look at Islam and the Christian Heresies of Arabia

Let's rewind a few hundred years before Islam, when Christianity was growing in the Roman Empire. During this time, there were many heretical groups that held differing beliefs about the identity of Jesus. Some questioned Jesus' humanity while others questioned his divinity. The orthodox Christian teaching is that Jesus is *both* fully man *and* fully God. Bishops, priests, and others who didn't hold to this belief were decreed heretics, and many of them fled east to Arabia to preach and evangelize. Their teachings left a palpable influence on Islam.

One such heretical group was the Arians who denied Jesus' divinity. Another group was the Nestorians who denied Jesus' humanity. There were also the Gnostics, who cast doubt on Jesus' Crucifixion.

An excellent example of how these groups influenced Islam can be found in the *Coptic Apocalypse of Peter*, a Gnostic text probably written in the 100s A.D. This apocryphal text (a text with doubtful authenticity) contains the following passage:

"The Savior said to me, 'He whom you saw on the tree, glad and laughing, this is the living Jesus. But this one into whose hands and feet they drive the nails is his fleshly part, which is the substitute being put to shame, the one who came into being in his likeness. But look at him and me.'"

The Gnostics believed that someone who was divine could not suffer or die—a belief that denies Jesus' humanity. Unwelcome in the Roman Empire, some Gnostics fled east to Arabia and brought the idea that a substitute died on the cross instead of Jesus himself.

By the end of the 6th century, at the time of Muhammad's birth, various influences—from the Byzantines to the Ethiopians to the Egyptian Copts—had touched Arabia. With major trading routes crossing through the region, Arabia was a diverse place inhabited by Arabs, Persians, Romans, Jews, Christians, pagans, and others. Of note, there were also growing movements that had become skeptical of Jesus' divinity in the region.

As a merchant, Muhammad encountered Christians, Jews, and people of other faiths. As early as the 8th century, a century after the beginning of Islam, St. John of Damascus—defending Christianity against the new Muslim conquerors of Syria—believed that Muhammad had likely come into contact with an Arian monk. Some scholars believe this Arian monk to actually have been the Nestorian monk Bahira who, according to Islamic tradition, met Muhammad in Syria and claimed to see in him the "sign of a prophet." Whatever the case, the Islamic belief about Jesus' crucifixion closely mirrors the confusion of the unorthodox Christian groups Muhammad encountered:

"And [for] their saying, 'Indeed, we have killed the Messiah, Jesus, the son of Mary, the messenger of Allah.' And they did not kill him, nor did they crucify him; but [another] was made to resemble him to them. And indeed, those who differ over it are in doubt about it. They have no knowledge of it except the following of assumption. And they did not kill him, for certain." (Quran, 4:157).

Just like in the *Coptic Apocalypse of Peter*, written about 500 years before the Quran, we see this idea that a substitute died on the cross. Except here the substitute's purpose is not to demonstrate that the divine cannot suffer, but to mirror a trend in Arabia, which rejected Jesus' divinity.

However, the substitute idea presents a new issue for Islam. If Jesus wasn't divine and a substitute was crucified in his place, what happened to the real Jesus? The Quran makes it even more complicated to iron out this logic by saying that Jesus was brought up to heaven instead of suffering crucifixion and there denies his divinity before God. This new addition to the substitute idea brings to mind several questions. Muslims believe God brought Jesus up to heaven so that a prophet wouldn't suffer unjustly. However, this argument goes against the Judeo-Christian tradition, in which prophets often suffered and died for preaching the truth—freely offering their lives for God. Jesus says, "Blessed are they who are persecuted for the sake of righteousness, for theirs is the kingdom of heaven" (Matt. 5:10). Why would God let other prophets die unjustly but save Jesus, especially if there was not some special relationship between Jesus and God? The Islamic account of the Crucifixion also doesn't account for why God would deceive onlookers into thinking that Jesus was crucified and only reveal otherwise 600 years later in the Quran. It does, however, demonstrate an awareness of the various Christian debates over the identity of Jesus that occurred in Arabia. In this context, the influence of Arabian heretical groups on the Quranic view of Jesus is clear.

In fact, certain Quranic verses only make sense in light of early Islam's contact with these groups. Although Islam denies that Jesus died and was resurrected from the dead, two verses in the Quran suggest otherwise. In the Quran, Jesus says, "Peace be upon me on the day I was conceived, and on the day on which I die, and on the day on which I come forth alive,"[2] (Quran, 19:33). Additionally, the Quran says that God told Jesus, "See, I will cause you to die, and I will cause you to fly to me" [3] (Quran, 3:55). Both of these verses says that Jesus will die and rise again—a belief that is unique to Christianity. They also contradict the Quranic account of Christ's Crucifixion, where Jesus is taken up to heaven but does not die and is not resurrected from the dead. These verses may also have served to mislead Christians into thinking Islam was compatible with Christianity and to encourage conversion to Islam.[4] However, orthodox Christians have always professed that Jesus truly died because his death affirms his humanity and that he was resurrected from the dead because his Resurrection confirms his true divinity. Thus, the contradictions in the Quran regarding Jesus only make sense in light of Christianity and invite us to look more closely at Jesus of Nazareth.

From a historical perspective, Muhammad took the idea of establishing (or re-establishing according to Islamic tradition) monotheism in Arabia too far—claiming to have received a new revelation that canceled out past revelations. Instead of adopting Judaism or Christianity, Muhammad presented a new religion with broad appeal to the peoples he conquered—one with fewer rules than Judaism and less radical beliefs that Christianity. But in covering the region under the banner of Islam, he and his followers also covered over pre-Islamic cultures, many of which held the truth to a major question the Quran does not answer: who is this man Jesus? The Quran says relatively little about Jesus other than that he performed miracles. To truly learn more about Christ, we have to turn to the Christian Scriptures, which chronicle his life, ministry, teaching, death, and resurrection. Jesus forgives sins—something only God can do, teaches on his own authority—rather than by Moses' (which is Jewish practice), heals the sick by his own power, fulfills the Jewish prophecies about the Messiah, and refers to himself as Lord of the Sabbath—a title reserved for God, the Creator of the Sabbath. Jesus says, "I am the light of the world" (Jn. 8:12) and "The Father [God] and I are one" (Jn. 10:30). From the New Testament, it's clear that Jesus is God made man who offers love, mercy, and redemption to all.

[2] The Arabic word for the translation "I come forth" used in the Quran is 'abᶜatha, which can also be translated "I am raised" or "I am resurrected" or "I am sent forth."

[3] The Arabic words used here are mutawffika and rafiᶜuka, meaning "I cause you to die" and "I raise you," respectively.

[4] Scholars are unanimous in the position that Muslims also forged a medieval document known as the Gospel of Barnabas, falsely attributed to the companion of St. Paul, which mirrored Islamic beliefs about Jesus and aimed at converting Christians to Islam.

The Quran and the Bible

The crux of the debate between Muslims and Christians lies in the differences in our holy texts. So, which text is more reliable? Before we get there, it's important to think about what one looks for to determine reliability. How do the texts demonstrate if they are true? What kind of investigation has been done into the truth of these documents? Could the original truth of something be lost in a train of witnesses? What reason might someone have for misleading others, whether intentionally or unintentionally? These are a few fair questions to ask.

Let's begin with the first question. The Bible (Old and New Testament) is the story of God's interaction with the human race. The Jews began to record their history in writing as God's Chosen People in Hebrew (and sometimes Aramaic) hundreds of years before Christ. They recorded the history of their people and God's covenant with them to bless them and bring the world to God through them in histories, instruction, prophecies, poems, psalms, and other forms of writing, which took place over the course of about two thousand years. Then came the birth of a Jewish man named Jesus, whom people claimed was divine. The four Gospels testify to Jesus' ministry, miracles, ability to forgive sins, and authority beyond the prophets — making clear the Christian belief that Jesus was God made man come to spread the good news of God's salvation.

The earliest Christian documents are actually St. Paul's letters, a Jewish man who persecuted the early Christians until he had a change of heart after encountering a blinding light and the voice of Jesus on the way to Damascus. The other books of the New Testament were written by Jesus' Apostles (a word meaning one who is sent with the authority of the one who sends) and disciples, and include the four Gospels as well as several other letters of instruction, counsel, and support to the early Christians. All of these texts, written over hundreds of years (most scholars estimate the New Testament itself was written in a period of about 100 years[5]) by people speaking Hebrew, Aramaic, and Greek would form a cohesive text known as the Bible — meaning Word [of God] in Greek. In total, considering the amazing fact that all of the books of the Bible form one coherent sum, there are at least as many testimonies to the truth of the Bible as there are books within it.

Muslims believe the Quran to be the eternal words of God, which cancel out all previous revelations. As a result, Muhammad is not seen as author of the Quran. However, Muslims believe the Quran was passed

---

[5] See *The New Testament* by Bart Ehrman.

down from Muhammad to others by oral tradition and then written down within a relatively short period of time—about half a century, according to historians. Yet, the Quran does not have the same sort of internal testimony that the Bible has. It rests on the testimony of one man. Furthermore, in rejecting the testimony of Jews and Christians, the Quran cuts itself off from the very tradition from which it claims its legitimacy.

The quick compilation of the Quran might seem to be an argument in its favor; however, there are important contradictions and inaccuracies within the text that suggest otherwise. For example, the Quran instructs Muslims to read what was written before it (referring to the Bible) but also says that it abrogates or cancels out all previous revelations. It also takes varying positions on how Muslims should treat non-Muslims with one passage instructing Muslims to kill all infidels. The majority of Classical Muslim scholars[6] accepted this passage (the final passage of the "verses of the sword") as the final position of God.[7] (While the majority of classical Muslim scholars believed unbelief a reason to declare war on other peoples, there is also a long tradition that believes war or lesser jihad to be a defensive response.) Muslim scholars have attempted to resolve this problem of internal contradictions with the practice of abrogation—taking what is believed to be the later revelation as true and regarding the former ones as null and void because any contradiction would cast doubt on the truth of the text. There are also historical inaccuracies in the Quran. The Quran confuses Mary, mother of Jesus, and Miriam, sister of Moses and Aaron, who lived hundreds of years apart. Ishmael is almost sacrificed by Abraham rather than Isaac. Also, Mary gives birth to Jesus by herself under a tree instead of with Joseph in Bethlehem. These internal contradictions and historical errors present an unanswered challenge to the authenticity of the Quran.

While critics of Christianity claim that the Bible also contains contradictions, Christians have always resolved these seeming contradictions through something called Sacred Tradition—which is the body of beliefs handed down by the Apostles through word of mouth and passed down through priests and bishops to the present day. Sacred Tradition is a way of understanding the Christian tradition that is inseparable from Scripture itself. Together, Sacred Tradition and Sacred Scripture form the Gospel: "Therefore, brothers, stand firm and hold fast to the traditions that you were taught, either by an oral statement or by a letter of ours," (2 Thes. 2:15). In light of Sacred Tradition, the seeming contradictions of Scripture are resolved. For example, while 1 Jn. 5:18 says that, "No one begotten by God sins," and Rom. 3:23 says, "All have

---

[6] The classical period of Islam refers to the 8th to 13th centuries.
[7] See *Jihad In Classical And Modern Islam* by Rudolph Peters.

sinned," Christians understand that all people sin, but it is God who grants us the grace to overcome human weakness. In this way, Sacred Tradition distinguishes Christianity from Islam by resolving seeming contradictions within the context of the preaching and teaching of the Apostles.

On the second question regarding investigation into the texts, the compilation of the New Testament was a moment of serious reflection on the Christian tradition. Each book was chosen based on whether it could be traced to Jesus' Apostles, whether it was used frequently in early liturgies throughout all the Churches, and whether it was believed to be inspired by God (in addition to other criteria).

As Muslims believe the Quran to be God's exact words, there has been no equivalent vetting process for the books of the Quran. In addition, Christian and atheist scholars have investigated the historicity of the Bible for centuries now. Many of these investigations have been hostile — intent on disproving Christian belief or attempting to radically modernize it. Yet, Christianity has withstood all of them. The Quran has not been subjected to this centuries long attempt to remove the supernatural from religious texts and in some cases to do away with religion itself.

Regarding the truth being changed by transmission over time, there certainly was more time for changes to be made to the Bible than to the Quran, as the Bible is much older. In fact, there are some small variations in early Christian manuscripts of the Bible. However, these were made by religious figures with the intent of preserving the tradition in which they were written and did not change the meaning of the text. On the other hand, the Quran was compiled relatively quickly. After Muhammad's death, varying Muslim factions used different verses or chapters to support their causes against each other and justify their right to rule. For this reason, one of the early Muslim caliphs (a political-religious leader) named 'Uthman ordered the compilation of one Quran and had all other variations burned — a well-documented fact even by Muslim historians. This is certainly a strange action, considering Muslims believe the Quran to be God's exact words and clearly brings to light a political motive. Despite this attempt to destroy variations in the Quran, some differing versions of the Quran still exist today, and while it is against Islam to believe that any part of the Quran has been changed over time, the early Muslims disagreed on the final version (more to come on this later). In addition, the oldest Qurans (some of which are still in existence) were written without dots (like the dot of an "i"), which can greatly change the meaning of a word in Arabic. Scholars debate the linguistic interpretation of this version, considering that the Arabic script developed from Aramaic. Thus, while the Quran was compiled faster than the Bible, the history behind it presents a political motive for changing a religious text aimed at amassing power.

Again, critics of Christianity claim the New Testament was compiled with political motives as well, in a way that would silence rival Christian groups. However, the New Testament books were written before Christianity entered into Roman politics and chosen based on the Apostolic Tradition, which originated hundreds of years before Christianity was legally tolerated in the Roman Empire. It is this Sacred Tradition that critics of Christianity tend to overlook in their arguments.

Lastly, is there any reason to mislead, intentionally or not? From the Jewish and Christian standpoints the answer is a firm no. The Jews have been the most persecuted people in history and they exercise great care and respect for the Tenakh (also called the Old Testament or Jewish Bible). If they really wanted to, they could have changed their beliefs so that they weren't persecuted. They could also have refused to record the multiple times many Jews turned away from God to worship false idols. Yet, they have kept these aspects of their history alive because they are true and a reminder that the House of Israel belongs to the Lord. Likewise, Christians were persecuted for centuries by the Romans and sometimes tortured for their faith. If Christians wanted to, they could have skipped the part about Jesus' divinity — which is a very radical belief coming from a Jewish background or dropped monotheism altogether.

The early Muslims experienced persecution in the city of Mecca for a short time, and so Muhammad left for a city called Medina. However, from there he would lead a group of his followers in conquering Mecca. From the start, Islam was entangled with politics. As mentioned, the reason the Quran was compiled so quickly was because competing Muslim groups made political claims to rule based on the parts of the Quran they possessed. Just like today, if there was any reason to mislead or possibility of miscommunication, it would most likely occur because of politics and not among small, persecuted groups recounting the history of their people and faith.

For these reasons and others, the Bible is the more trustworthy religious text. The fact that it was written over hundreds of years by various inspired authors and yet remains internally coherent demonstrates it is more reliable. The Quran on the other hand contains internal contradictions and historical inaccuracies and rests on the testimony of one man. Scholars have subjected the Bible to intense historical scrutiny while the Quran has not undergone a similar process. The Old Testament was compiled by the Jewish rabbis and the New Testament was compiled according to particular standards by religious authorities; whereas, the Quran was compiled in the context of warring Muslim factions who used individual books to support their own political claims. Lastly, persecuted Christians and Jews had little reason to deceive while Muslim political groups fought with each other and then went on to conquer other peoples — tying Islam to the dangerous web of politics from its inception.

The Spread of Islam

Please see Ira M. Lapidus' Islamic Societies to the Nineteenth Century and Jihad in Classical and Modern Islam by Rudolph Peters for supporting and additional information.

While the period of Western imperialism lasted roughly from soon after the discovery of the New World in 1492 to the mid-1900s, the period of Islamic imperialism that preceded it lasted roughly from the mid-600s to modern times. It's hard for many people today to imagine a time when Europe was the victim of imperialism. However, it's crucial to explore this period in order to understand Islam's origins and beliefs.

The violent spread of Islam represents a major reason why it cannot be true, as a truthful religion doesn't need to impose itself by force. While Muslims see the early Muslim military victories as miraculous proof in favor of Islam, the resultant unprovoked violence, death of innocents, enslavement, and war brought about the near extinction of ancient cultures that preceded Islam by thousands of years. Such cultures — the Aramaic-speaking Assyrians and Chaldeans, the ancient Egyptians (Copts), the Phoenicians and other groups that had adopted Christianity — left an indelible but purposefully unrecognized mark on modern Arab culture. Today, Muslims, Jews, Christians, and others recognize acts like these, which began with Muhammad himself, as crimes against humanity.

Born in the city of Mecca in the late 500s A.D., Muhammad claimed to have received revelations from the angel Gabriel, which cancelled out all the Jewish and Christian revelations that came before. Initially, his preaching was not well received, so he fled to the city of Medina. There, he gained followers and converts, with whom he conquered his hometown of Mecca. Afterwards, he destroyed all the pagan Arab idols in the city's religious shrine and claimed it was the place where Abraham had built an altar (although Mecca is very far from ancient Israel). Pilgrimages to this shrine were a major part of its pagan pre-Islamic past and continue today as one of Islam's main practices. Muhammad would go on to conquer much of the Arabian Peninsula, solidifying his power in Mecca and putting dissenters to the sword. After his death in the mid-600s, the early Muslims would conquer from the west of India to Spain by the early 700s.

To put this massive conquest into historical context, the main empires of the day — the Byzantine Empire and the Persian Empire — were weakened after centuries of fighting. The new Islamic conquests would see war, destruction, enslavement, and the subordination of Christian populations who made up a significant part of the population in the

Levant, Iraq, Egypt, and North Africa to their Muslims conquerors. Jews and Christians were allowed to continue practicing their religions, but they had to pay an extra tax stipulated in the Quran, called the *jizyah* tax, and follow certain restrictions. However, if they were too poor to pay (and most people of the time lived in poverty), then they could leave (which was hard to do if you were poor), convert, or die. People of other faiths only had the option of converting, leaving, or execution. Public displays of non-Muslim religion, like processions, were banned and various other laws existed to enshrine the lesser status of the conquered native peoples.

Lesser Jihad

Only 150 years after the Islamic conquest would Muslim scholars put forth the first concept of jihad in an attempt to justify the horrible violence committed. The Arabic word *jihad* is often translated to mean, "striving in the way of Allah," and Muslim scholars distinguish between greater jihad — an internal striving on the part of the individual, and lesser jihad — the often collective duty of Muslims to propagate Islam through war. Muslim scholars have never agreed on one definition for or set of circumstances that justify lesser jihad, although Islam's classical period sheds a bit more light on the topic. This period, which lasted between the 8th and 13th centuries, is seen as the high point of Islamic civilization and thought and therefore carries great influence on Islam through the present day. The classical scholars ranged from more defensive to more bellicose understandings of jihad, with the majority believing that unbelief in Islam constituted a form of aggression that justified a collective duty by Muslims to wage war against non-Muslims. According to their worldview, which was adopted from the pagan Arabs, all civilizations lived in a perpetual state of war. Dying in the fight to spread Islam — the Islamic concept of martyrdom — was and is highly esteemed. Although, Modernist Muslims accept modern international norms and interpret lesser jihad as a means to defend Islam (rather than to offensively attack), they form a minority of Muslims worldwide. It's also unclear why they favor certain peaceful verses in the Quran instead of the final verse of the sword accepted by the classical scholars, which commanded the killing of disbelievers. Muhammad, himself, was clear on the topic of lesser jihad. In one hadith, when a man asked about how to attain the highest place in paradise, Muhammad replied "Jihad in the way of Allah!" Thus, while there are different interpretations of lesser jihad, the origins of this concept and the classical scholars ' opinions make it clear that the virulently violent jihad seen today — even if not all Muslims accept or participate in it — is part and parcel of Islam's history.

Islamic Expansion Outside Arabia: A Few Examples

Islamic societies over the centuries were unique in their usage of slave soldiers to uphold the defense of dynasties and empires. From very early on in Islamic history, conquered or captured people were enslaved as soldiers to fight for the Muslim powers of the day. Turks and central Asians, valued for their fighting prowess, were captured and made into slave soldiers (many Turks and central Asians would later convert to Islam). Slave soldiers had significant power in Islamic societies because of their important role, often receiving the ability to collect taxes from a particular area—an institution know as the *iqta'*. Slaves who converted to Islam would be made freemen. In the 1200s A.D., the slave soldiers of Egypt became so powerful that they overthrew the leaders and established the Mamluk Empire (the Arabic word *mamluk* means owned or slave). Slave military forces were essential to the Ottoman Turks, who largely took them from the European Balkan states they had conquered beginning in the 1300s A.D. European pressure on the Ottoman Empire would later lead to the extinction of slavery in much of the Middle East and North Africa. However, it still continues in some Islamic societies today.

After the initial Islamic conquest of the 600s and 700s, the Muslim Turks would go on to further their military gains. Blending the Islamic notion of lesser jihad and Turkish notions of fighting, Turkish warriors or *ghazis* (from the Arabic word *ghazu*, meaning to invade) would win the Battle of Manzikert in 1071 against the Byzantine Empire. This would open Anatolia—one of the earliest regions to adopt Christianity through the peaceful preaching of St. Paul and others—to a wave of Turkish migrations westward and centuries of fighting that eventually ended in the consolidation of a Turkish Muslim state in a land where Turks were previously foreigners. In 1451, the Turks would take Constantinople, the crowning jewel and capital of the Christian Byzantine Empire for over 1,000 years, converting its main church, the *Hagia Sophia* (meaning holy wisdom in Greek), into a mosque. The Turks would extend their military gains all the way to Hungary and Romania to the Ukraine and the Balkan states. Greece would remain under Ottoman control until the 19th century. At the same time, there was less pressure to convert in Ottoman-controlled Europe and less of an influx of Turks into the region. Anatolia, however, would lose Greek culture, language, and Christianity, as only very small Christian populations exist in Turkey today.

Muslim-conquered Spain presents another important window into the Islamic conquest. While many scholars hail the advances of Muslim society in Spain—which lasted in various parts of the country from 711A.D. to 1492A.D.—it's often overlooked that if the Muslim Moors had had their way, there would be no Spain today. Spaniards would be in a similar situation to that of the stateless Palestinians in modern times. Due to varying divisions, the Islamic Caliphate of Cordoba (in modern Spain) eventually collapsed and was divided into multiple smaller regions. This allowed for the Christians in Northern Spain to retake their land and begin the long process of the Reconquista or the re-conquest of their native land. While the Spanish did expel the Jews and Muslims after Granada fell to the Christian Spanish in 1492, they did so in the context of just having regained their own land from people who attacked them without provocation and carried out at least two instances of forced conversions among Christians and Jews.

Muslim expansion in Africa presents another important case study. Some African-Americans have converted to Islam because they believed their ancestors to have been Muslim, but Islam was imposed on Africa as well. While Europeans bought African slaves to bring them to the New World, slavery had been nearly extinct in Western Europe for about 500 years prior to Columbus' discovery;[8] it was often Muslims who had conquered African peoples, supplied, and sold them. After the conquest of Northern Africa by the Arabs, Islam in Africa spread primarily through the migration of Muslim merchants, teachers, and settlers. Migration in order to spread Islam is considered a form of jihad. Alongside this strain of non-violent colonization, was also the militant aim of turning these small Muslim settlements in Africa into Muslim states and conquering the infidels. The results of the jihads of the 18th and 19th century in Western Africa can still be seen today in the emergence of the terrorist organization Boko Haram (meaning Western education is forbidden) in Nigeria—a group which has killed more Christians than the Islamic State of Iraq and Syria (ISIS). West African jihads lead to the enslavement of thousands who would serve in the army, administration, and as concubines and domestic servants. Much of the western and central Sudan was enslaved as the result of Muslim conquests and rule. Eastern Africa had a robust slave trade, with Zanzibar eventually developing into the center of the international slave trade. These slaves were traded throughout the Islamic societies of the world and beyond. In Senegambia, the wars between the traditional warrior elites and the Muslim jihadists would promote slavery, as the demand for slaves grew from the Atlantic slave trade. Scholars estimate that about 20-30% of Africans that came to the Americas were Muslims.[9] This does not necessarily mean they were educated in Islam. Islam often blended with traditional African beliefs to varying degrees on the African continent. The conversion of these slaves to Islam may also

---

[8] See *The Medieval World* by Dorsey Armstrong.
[9] According to a professor of Middle Eastern and South Asian Languages and Cultures at the University of Virginia

have been the result of Muslim settlements or jihads establishing Islamic law, which forbids polytheistic practices and punishes disbelievers with death. A key takeaway here is that Muslim Arabs and Muslim Africans enslaved Africans who practiced their traditional beliefs and sold them on the international slave market. Muslim societies also stood to gain from the lucrative African slave trade, which was begun by the Arabs in the 11th century and would come to extend from the Americas to Indonesia.

Islamic Imperialism in Modern Times

Given these examples and this very brief history, it's more than fair to say that Christians have suffered more at the hands of Islamic imperialism than Muslims have suffered at the hands of European imperialism—which was often less religious than nationalistic in nature. After all, Syria, Lebanon, Jordan, Israel/Palestine, Iraq, Egypt, North Africa, and Turkey—all part of the ancient Roman Empire—once contained significant Christian populations or majorities as a result of peaceful preaching and evangelization.

Sadly, the violence of the past has not left us as Muslim aggression against Christians and others continues in modern times. Turkey committed genocide against Christian Armenians and other Christian groups in 1915, exterminating around 1-2 million people in a land that was once majority Christian. Turkey still holds on to Constantinople—a city comparable to Rome for Roman Catholics to the Greek Orthodox—even though it was supposed to be given back to the Greeks after World War I (in which the Ottomans fought on the side of Germany and lost). In the late 1900s, Turkey invaded Cyprus for the second time—a land evangelized by St. Paul, one of the Apostles—and retains significant influence on part of the island today. As late as 2017, Turkish President Erdogan publicly told Turkish Muslims living in Europe that they were "the future of Europe," and encouraged them to have several children in order to populate the West.

The Saudi government teaches an even more fundamentalist form of Islam, called Wahabism, and exports these intolerant beliefs throughout the world. All non-Islamic houses of worship are banned on Saudi soil, and government textbooks teach that Christians and Jews are enemies of Islam. ISIS used these very textbooks in its short-lived caliphate in Iraq and Syria, while it committed another genocide against Christians, Yezidis, and other religious minorities in the Middle East.

Egyptian society discriminates against Coptic Christians, disadvantaging them economically and politically, while the government does not do enough to prevent the seizure of Coptic lands by Muslim neighbors or the capture of Christian girls. Many people accuse Egyptian

Al-Azhar University, the preeminent Sunni Islamic educational institution, for also exporting intolerance and jihad.

Islamic terrorist groups are located in every Islamic nation throughout the world as well as in non-Islamic nations, as we have seen in the horror of September 11th and the multiple terrorist attacks carried out throughout Europe. *Boko Haram and Muslim Fulani herdsman are currently committing genocide against Christians in Nigeria today.* Their religiously motivated violence has resulted in more deaths than ISIS' attempt to eradicate ancient Christian communities that predate Islam by hundreds of years. Pakistan uses its blasphemy laws to target and execute Christians. Christians have all but left Gaza, the West Bank, and Israel — the birthplace of Christianity itself. These horrific events and others have led to the mass exodus of Christians from the Middle East — and the Christian population, which was approximately 20% of the Middle East at the beginning of the 20th century, now stands at less than 5%. While many Western academics may have chosen to view this religious violence through a whitewashed, secular lens, such violence is in keeping with the history of Islamic expansion.

Final Thoughts

It's important to understand this little-known history because it reminds us that imperialism is not uniquely European — it's a *human* problem. It also offers a deeper understanding of Islamic history and society, specifically how the concept of jihad has been used to justify wars, conquests, and enslavements against those viewed as infidels. At the same time, knowledge of this history, while upsetting, should not foment hatred. Rather, it should inspire an even greater outpouring of love towards our Muslim brothers and sisters because they do not know the true peace Christ offers. While there are various Muslim actors who impose their religion on others, many Muslims simply want a good life for themselves and their children. Christ taught us to love those who hate us and to pray for those who persecute us. This divine teaching — the offering of love to both friend and enemy alike — is what distinguishes Christianity, and we ought to share this message with the world, especially at a time when Muslim emigration to Western nations has led to growing Muslim populations in Europe reaching about 7-9% in France and 5% in most major European nations.

In response to the violence of certain Muslim actors and the indifference of secular governments, we Christians — no matter our denomination — must stand in solidarity and dedicate ourselves all the more to our Christian duty of sharing the Good News of Jesus Christ. It is illegal to evangelize in Muslim societies; however, we now have an opportunity to share the Gospel of life with them so that they can share the love of Christ with their family and friends and perhaps revive our Christian faith in the land of its birth and grow the Body of Christ throughout the world.

Christians, Jews, and other groups have greatly suffered over the centuries due to Islamic imperialism—ranging from persecution to colonization to death in battle to the Ottoman slave trade of Christians. While there were certainly injustices committed during the Crusades and the period of modern European colonialism, these eras represent a much shorter timespan than that of Islamic imperialism—which extends from the beginning of Islam to the present day. In addition, it's important to recognize that the efforts of Europeans also led to the extinction of slavery in Europe and the Ottoman Empire as well as to the international norms condemning imperialism and conquest. With everything that people believe today about the evils of imperialism, slavery, and the dangers of mixing politics and religion, how can we view a religion that immediately entered into politics and war upon its inception and imposed itself upon other peoples as credible? God saved the Israelites from slavery in Egypt and granted the early Roman Christians perseverance under great persecution and pressure. Our Creator does not need war and violence to manifest His Truth; He made this known when He came to us in the form of a poor defenseless infant from Bethlehem.

Did You Know?

As Muslims believe the Jewish and Christians Scriptures were corrupted, it can be hard to introduce them to Christ based on the Bible or historical knowledge alone. That's why it's important to have at least a few main points from the Islamic sources themselves to demonstrate the holes in Islam and the truth of Christianity. Please also know that disputing the trustworthiness of the Quran or Muhammad, even using Islamic sources, can be considered very sensitive among Muslims. A few main places to start the discussion might begin with a well-intentioned did you know...

The Quran points to the divinity of Christ?

Many parts of the Quran don't make sense without the Judeo-Christian background Islam rejected. That's why, even though Islam denies Christ's divinity, in the Quran:

- The name of Jesus is mentioned more frequently than Muhammad's.
- God commands Muhammad and his followers to read the Jewish and Christian Scriptures when they have doubts (Quran 10:94).
- Jesus performs miracles and healings, but Muhammad does not.
- God speaks of Jesus' Resurrection, even though Islam rejects it (Quran 3:55; 19:33).
- Jesus is the only person in the Quran said to be without sin (Quran 19:19).

The Quran has changed over time?

The Quran was compiled in the context of warring Muslim factions claiming the right to rule based on the parts of the Quran they had. The Islamic sources themselves, as well as the later standardization of the Arabic script, make it clear that the Quran has changed over time.

- Muhammad's top Quran reciters disagreed on the compilation of the Quran (Ibn Sa'd, *Kitab at-Tabaqat al-Kabir*, vol. 2, p. 444).
- The Caliph 'Uthman compiled one copy of the Quran in the mid 600s A.D. and burned all varying copies (Sahih al-Bukhari, 6.61.150).
- Ibn 'Umar, a companion of Muhammad, records: "Much of the Quran has been lost," (as-Suyuti, *al-Itqan fi 'Ulum al-Qur'an*).

- The oldest Quran in existence is written without dots that change a word's meaning in Arabic.
- The standardization of the Arabic script occurred centuries after the Quran was written, which could lead to different understandings of its meaning.

About the life of Muhammad?

According to Ibn Ishaq's *Sirat Rasul Allah*, the first and most authoritative Islamic biography on the life of Muhammad, Muhammad instigated violent raids and battles, committed acts of cruelty — including against women and children, and took part in and permitted his men to take women from the towns they conquered. In this biography, Muhammad:

- Engaged in offensive raids before conquering his native town (Mecca) and in one instance beheaded 100 men in a day. He also attacked towns that did not accept his message, based on whether they had built mosques or not.
- Massacred a Jewish tribe in the town of Khaybar and sold the women and children into slavery.
- Ordered the killing of a breastfeeding mother in front of her children for speaking against Islam.
- Was seized with fear at the visit of the Angel Gabriel and attempted suicide multiple times afterwards.
- Claimed to be possessed after he told the early Muslims they could pray to three goddesses (also in the Quran).
- Married more than the permitted four wives, which he enjoined on his followers, and claimed that God wanted one of his companions to divorce his wife so Muhammad could marry her instead. One of Muhammad's wives, 'Aishah — whom he married at six years old, consummating the marriage at nine years old — claimed Muhammad's revelations suited his desires.
- Ibn Ishaq states he left out disturbing parts of Muhammad's biography.

Islamic and Christian Views on God

The way Muslims and Christians view God represents a major distinction between the two religions. While adherents of both faiths believe God is all-powerful, omniscient, and omnipresent, the God of Islam is utterly unapproachable and beyond humanity whereas the God of Christianity is intimately involved in a world he seeks to draw to Himself. It is only the God of Jesus Christ who loves His creation and desires the good of each person.

The God of the Quran is very like an earthly king. He has no commitment, can contradict Himself and always be right (the Islamic belief in abrogation), can predestine people to heaven or hell, and He is totally above all. In Islam, God can never be known and union with God even in heaven is considered blasphemy. The Islamic view of heaven is a place of paradise, but still a place where God is not intimately present and known among those who love Him—in fact, love of God is not commanded in Islam. Thus, while Muslim scholars might say that Christians put limitations on God by saying that God became man and loves all people (a form of commitment that the limitless God can't be held to), in a sense, Islam humanizes God more so than Christianity by making Him into nothing more than a human ruler.

Christians believe that God is Love—not that God is *like* love or even that God loves humanity in some general way—but that God *is* Love and desires the reconciliation of all people to Himself. This is the Good News that Jesus came to share with us: God is our loving Father, and if we follow His commands, we will remain in His Love for eternity. God does not act like an earthly king. Rather, he is *better than any king we can imagine*: intimately involved in the world and desiring the salvation of all people. For this reason, the goal of Christianity is so much more than what any other religion offers. Jesus offers *communion* with God—living completely in union with God's Will and filled with every heavenly grace and blessing. In this sense, the Good News of Christianity is truly unique. God, Who is Love, loves us and desires us to return to communion with Him with all of our hearts that He may transform us and grant us His salvation.

In comparing Islamic and Christian views of God, it's clear that the message of Islam is not as good as the Good News Jesus came to share. The One, True God became man, preached the coming of the Kingdom of God, suffered for our sins, died, and was raised again from the dead to teach us that through every cross and burden, through dying to the ways of the world, there is a resurrection to new life in Him who is Our Savior and God. The love of God that Christ proclaimed, which is in our hearts, which we have experienced in our lives, and which defines us as His followers is what we must share with our Muslim neighbors. While mere words and arguments can be tossed aside, God's love draws all people to the truth.

Introducing Christianity

A Brief Introduction

God, the Lord of all Creation, desires an intimate relationship with each person He has created. As our Eternal Father, He created us out of a superabundance of His Love—in perfect communion with Him and one another. When Adam and Eve turned away from God in the Garden of Eden, they destroyed that communion and brought about both a physical and spiritual Fall from the paradise God intended us to inhabit. As their descendants—as human beings, we can never truly make up for this original sin because there is nothing that we can give to God that He does not already have. In His time, and in His Way, God redeemed us. He became man in the person of Jesus Christ and preached the coming of God's Kingdom. In dying on the cross, Jesus, as man, offered the sacrifice of his own Body for all of humanity, and as God, was capable of doing something humanity could not do—reconcile man to God. This is the Good News of Jesus Christ—that God the Father has sent the Son to give salvation to all the world, to all who love and follow Him through the Holy Spirit.

The following chapters explain elements of our faith that are unique to Christianity—beliefs that we need to share with each other, our Muslim neighbors, and the world so that all people might know the eternal truth and abiding love of Christ. Islamic societies reject the Christian understanding of God and His Divine Love. So, let us readily share the reason for our hope, the joy of Christ, and the love of God—living out our call to Christian charity and striving towards a Christian culture that draws all who encounter it into the Most Sacred Heart of Jesus.

"Then Jesus approached and said to them, 'All power in heaven and on earth has been given to me. Go, therefore, and make disciples of all nations, baptizing them in the name of the Father, and of the Son, and of the holy Spirit, teaching them to observe all that I have commanded you. And behold, I am with you always, until the end of the age,'" (Matt. 28:18-20).

How Could a Man be God?

It's hard to wrap our head around the idea that God could become human. On its face, it seems like a fairly silly idea. On the one hand, we can't say that God *cannot* become man because this would limit the limitless God. On the other hand, we might ask why God would choose to become human and enter into our imperfect, sinful society.

St. Anselm, an Italian monk from the Middle Ages, offers a beautiful explanation as to why God would become man. He says that in the beginning, humanity (Adam and Eve) sinned against God but was incapable of atoning for that sin (after all, how can humans ever give something to God through repentance that He does not already have?). As a result, it was necessary for a divine person to make atonement in humanity's place—thus, God, not out of necessity but out of Love, became man to do what we cannot do on our own: make up for our sins.

If you're still not convinced, the New Testament offers further reason to believe otherwise. In the Gospels[10], you'll notice a few things that seem odd for a human to do or say. For one, Jesus teaches with his own authority. This would have been very strange to a first century Jew, where teachers claimed authority from their teachers all the way back to Moses. Another odd element of the Gospels is all of Jesus' miracles. No prophet in recorded history performed so many miracles in his *own* name (rather than God's). Jesus also asks people to believe not only in his teachings but also in *him*. If we read this in context it will make sense that Jesus has some special relationship with God above any other human person. For this reason, he calls God his Father, which was rather unusual at that time. Jesus also forgives sins—something only God can do, beyond the power of any prophet. In addition, Jesus says he is one with God. Even though Jesus never explicitly says "I am God," it is clear from reading the Gospels that Jesus, through various signs and statements, claims to be the Son of God and thus God Himself.

---

[10] To read the Gospels free online, see the United States Conference of Catholic Bishops website: **https://bible.usccb.org/bible**. The word Gospel means Good News, and each Gospel account is a testimony written by Jesus' Apostles and disciples about what they saw and heard in their lifetimes about the life of Jesus. Matthew, Mark, and Luke—the Synoptic Gospels (synoptic meaning "seen together")—are very similar in their telling of the teachings of Jesus. The Gospel of John is much more theological than the others, demonstrating profound spiritual reflection on the life and teaching of Jesus.

It seems crazy that God would become man. Yet, if we understand this within God's plan of returning us to communion with Him, it doesn't seem so illogical. "God is Love" (1 John 4:8). God loves humanity and desires the salvation of *all* people. And so God has shown us how to return to communion with Him by believing in and imitating His Son.

The Holy Trinity

Christians believe that the Trinity is something beyond our ability to fully understand in this life. Nonetheless, we received this understanding of a Triune God from the divine revelation preserved in Sacred Tradition and recorded in the Scriptures, and it's important to understand what this concept means for Christians.

First, we have to understand something about love, what St. Thomas Aquinas defines as willing the good of the other. No other religion claims that God *is* Love. But what exactly does love entail? Love involves one who loves, one who is loved, and the love between them. Even though there are three parts to love, it is still Love—indivisible, unified, and unifying. In a similar manner, God is Father: the One who loves, Son: the One who is loved, and Holy Spirit: the love between them—indivisible, unified, and unifying. According to Christianity, God is a Divine Communion of Love, One God in three Persons, Who calls all people into the relationship of His Love.

That God is Love means that Christianity is all about Love—willing the good of others, uniting ourselves and all that we have to God. Love unifies—and God, as Love, seeks to unite all of His creation to Himself, to invite humanity into His Own interior life of Love and perfect communion. Christianity is all about opening ourselves to and participating in God's Love so that we become holy through it.

That God is Triune means that God presents us with a model of love for our families and relationships. Out of the love of a man and woman comes the love between them: their child. Out of love between friends comes lasting joy. God's love is unconditional—beyond conditions that might limit it. This means that just as God wills the world to return to communion with Him, we too ought to love our friends and enemies alike—willing their good, praying for them, and in so doing participating in God's Divine Love and Life.

The Goal of Christianity: Communion with God

Belief in Jesus as the Son of God changed religion itself forever and makes Christianity unique. No other faith claims that the only God took on flesh to save His Chosen People (the Jews) and through them all peoples (the Gentiles). This is the Good News of Christ—that even though humanity turned away from God in the Garden of Eden by sinning and continues to do so today, God still seeks out communion with us. The story of God's efforts to bring us back to Him: the covenant with Abraham, the establishment of Israel, the slavery of the Hebrews in Egypt, their return to Israel, the prophets, kings, and judges, and eventually the new covenant of Jesus—this is what Christians refer to as salvation history. God became man to encounter us in our limited nature, our transgressions, our errors, and our disunity and to promise us everlasting life and peace if we live in and for Him, in total abandonment to His Will (something that may resonate with Muslims who seek submission to God's Will). Christians do not believe that God became man and then stepped back from our world to let it carry on as it pleases. Rather, our God is a personal God—a God Who has always interacted with His creation—Who seeks to reunite us, the human race, with Himself.

But what does this reunion look like? Is it some vague notion of eternal happiness in heaven? Is it some purely spiritual realm where we will be more aware of God's presence? No—it's much more! The Christian faith is the only religion that professes that those in heaven will live *in communion with God*. This state of communion is beyond what our words can describe, but in this state we will live in complete communion with God and our neighbor in a more elevated state than that of Adam and Eve in the Garden of Eden. We will be *made whole* (the definition of salvation from Latin) in our God—trusting in and depending on Him fully, needing nothing and wanting for nothing but Our Creator and living in perfect serenity. No longer will we be unable to fully communicate with each other. In a state of full communion there will be no arguments, no distrust, no bitterness or anxiety. There will be no jealousy or fighting or death. Communion with God is a participation in the Divine.

Christians often say that Christ became man so that our humanity could participate in His divinity. As a result of God becoming man, He showed us how we ought to live truly as human beings. In other words, Jesus showed us authentic humanity—what humanity was meant to be. Again, I can't stress enough how inadequate our words are to describe this communion—but this is the end of our earthly pilgrimage: communion (literally meaning *union with*) with our Lord Who makes us whole and allows us to participate in His Divine Life.

Redemptive Suffering and Love

For many people, Christian and non-Christian alike, the idea that suffering can be redemptive is difficult to understand. Yet, because Jesus offered himself as a reparation offering for the sins of the world, because he did what humankind could not do—taking our place on the cross as man and atoning for our sins with the fullness of his power as God—the earliest Christians understood that by uniting our sufferings to Christ's sufferings on the cross as an offering and prayer, God, in His mercy, allows human beings to participate in the redemption of the world. After every cross of suffering, there is a resurrection to new life. The Resurrection of Jesus from the dead—that moment which confirmed the divine truth of Jesus' ministry—affirms this for us. Suffering itself, suffering—which we so often see as defeat or an instrument of the devil to turn us away from God's commandments—is transformed into the greatest act of love on the cross of Christ. For this reason Jesus tells us, "Do no be afraid; just have faith" (Mk. 5:36).

In Christianity, suffering is never meaningless. Rather, as St. Teresa of Calcutta says, it is exactly in our sufferings and humiliations that we draw closest to Jesus at the Crucifixion. It is there, at the foot of the cross with Mary, his mother, and St. John that we behold the face of God with hands outstretched that he might embraces us, kiss us, and say, "I love you."

And just as Jesus died for the whole world, Christians are called to live with this same humility and self-sacrificial love towards all people—Muslims, Jews, other Christians, and all those we encounter. It is no surprise that Jesus teaches us, "No one has greater love than this, to lay down one's life for one's friends" (Jn. 15:13), and again, "Whoever wishes to be great among you shall be your servant; whoever wishes to be first among you shall be your slave," (Matt. 20:26-27). Yet, Jesus makes it clear that we should not seek to be last simply for glory—no, Christians seek to be the servants of all because it's pleasing to God. Christians seek to be last because we believe that by offering our gifts, talents, blessings, sufferings—all that we have and all that we are—in total abandonment to the Divine Will, we can participate in the salvation of the world because this pleases the One True God, Author of Life and Creator of the World.

The Most Blessed Sacrament

God became man out of his Divine Love for humanity, and when He accomplished his salvific mission on the cross, died, and rose again, He did not leave us alone to await the Second Coming of Jesus and Judgment Day. Instead, he instituted the Sacraments that we might know His Love until the end of time. A sacrament is a visible sign of an invisible reality—a sign that communicates God's abiding presence and love. When received in humility, a sacrament lifts up the human spirit to God, draws us into the Divine Life, and invites us to enter into the Ocean of God's Mercy. There are Seven Sacraments, which are also referred to as the Seven Mysteries because they draw us into the mystery of God and conform us into the very image of Jesus himself by strengthening us to choose the good of His commandments. All those who belong to the Body of Christ, the Church, receive these beautiful, freely given gifts of God. That's why it's so important to talk about what Catholics call the Most Blessed Sacrament.

On the night before Judas Iscariot handed Jesus over to the Jewish and Roman authorities, Christ established a New Covenant with humankind—the covenant all creation had awaited, that all people might worship the One True God through his Chosen People Israel. On this night, at the Last Supper, "the Lord Jesus...took bread, and, after he had given thanks, broke it and said, 'This is my body that is for you. Do this in remembrance of me.' In the same way also the cup, after supper, saying, 'This cup is the new covenant in my blood. Do this, as often as you drink it, in remembrance of me.' For as often as you eat this bread and drink the cup, you proclaim the death of the Lord until he comes,' (1 Cor. 11:23-26). These are the same words Catholic priests proclaim today in the celebration of the Eucharist—a word that means true thanksgiving; and we give thanks because Jesus Christ remains truly present with us today in the blessed bread and wine of the Eucharist. At the Last Supper, Jesus takes the place of the Passover sacrifice—the sacrifice that spared the Hebrews from God's vengeance on Egypt during their enslavement—and prefigures his sacrifice on the cross. For this reason, Jesus is called the Lamb of God, offered for the sins of the world; he fulfills the Jewish Covenant and invites all people to share in the salvation of God.

In the Eucharist, Christ invites us to receive his Body and so become a member of it—a member of the Church—in the ultimate sign of unity. When we receive the Eucharist at Mass, we behold the endless love of God poured out to and offered for the world. There, in that bread and wine, God nourishes us with the food of angels that we might conform ourselves to His very image, the image of His Son, and abandon our will that we might seek His. Beholding His holiness, God asks us to empty ourselves of our attachments and sins that He might fill our hearts with his love, so we might share His Love with the world. This is the glory of the Eucharistic feast. This is why the Eucharist is truly considered the Most Blessed Sacrament.

The Communion of Saints

The word saint, from Latin, means holy, and a saint is someone who's made it to heaven. The saints are those people who loved God on earth, who cooperated with His grace, who found favor with Him, and who led exemplary Christian lives. Catholics believe that all people are called to communion with each other and to God in heaven—in what is called the Communion of Saints. The Church recognizes certain individuals as saints because they provide examples to follow for Christians all over the world.

Christians believe that the Church is one in heaven and on earth, and so at the moment of death, we don't cease to be a member of Christ's Body. Rather, purified from our sins and united to God, we'll have the clarity to see the world as it truly is and to understand how deeply it needs God's healing love and light. In heaven, even though we may no longer need to pray for ourselves, we'll continue to pray for those on earth because it's the calling of every Christian—and every person—to participate in God's redemption of the world. For this reason, we often entrust our prayers to the intercession of the saints in heaven.

Sacred Tradition has always affirmed Mary's unique intercessory role as Mother of God and Mother of the Church. God chose to enter into the world through her, and in all humility she responded, "Behold, I am the handmaid of the Lord. May it be done to me according to your word," (Lk. 1:38). Mary found favor with God, she gave birth to Jesus, raised him, was present with him at his death, and witnessed his Ascension into heaven. This is why Mary has a special place in the heart and spirituality of the Church. Mary participated in a unique way in God's salvific mission on earth and continues to do so in heaven today by drawing others into a relationship with her Son.

Just as we might ask our friends on earth to pray for us, we also ask the saints in heaven for their intercession before God. We entrust our prayers to our brothers and sisters who have run the race and emerged victorious—not because they come between us and God, but because they can present our petitions before the divine throne in light of their communion with our Lord in heaven.

The Universality of the Catholic Faith

The word catholic means universal, and the Catholic Church is a universal Church not only because it seeks to share the Gospel with the world but because of the great diversity within it. The beauty of this diversity expressed within the context of Christian communion attests to the truth of our faith. Unlike the expansion of Islam, which led to the Arabization of the Middle East and the extinction of native cultures, the early Christians sought to draw each culture they came into contact with to Christ. As a result, different rites developed within the Church.

A rite is a tradition of how the Sacraments are celebrated, and there are 24 rites within the Catholic Church. Most people are familiar with the Latin rite (Roman Catholicism); yet, there are other forms of Catholicism that share the same Sacraments, priesthood, and beliefs. Catholics of any rite can worship together and receive the Eucharist in each other's Churches. We can also draw hope from the unity among our rites. While each rite has a unique set of traditions, customs, history, language, and a distinct liturgy, each professes the same eternal truths. In this way, the 24 rites display the beautiful diversity of the Christian heritage. Just as Latin is the official language of the Latin rite, Greek is the official language of the Byzantine Greek Catholic Church, and Syriac (a later form of Aramaic, the language Jesus spoke) is the official language of the Maronite Catholic Church; Coptic Catholics use Coptic (a form of ancient Egyptian) and Ukrainian Catholics use Old Slavonic. The early Christians saw that there is good in every culture, as Jesus came to redeem all peoples. And so, the Church extends through different regions, cultures, and peoples — unified in their diversity, which testifies to the truth of their shared, universal beliefs.

The Persecuted Church

Christianity is currently the most persecuted religion in the world. Christians have always born persecution from groups within and outside their societies—from the days of ancient Rome to the Islamic conquest to the rise of nationalism and secularism throughout the world. Today Christians suffer for the name of Jesus in North Korea, China, the Middle East, Africa, and even in Europe and the Americas. For this reason it's curious that Tertullian, an influential second-century Christian writer from Carthage (modern-day Tunisia), would have thought to write, "The blood of the martyrs is the seed of the Church." After all, how can suffering persecution actually lead to the growth of the Church? I believe it is because persecution makes visible the divine love of Christ present in his Church. This love—which is a sacred mystery beyond human comprehension—is something all Christians seek to reflect into the world.

After having read this booklet, you may still be wondering why this discussion of Islam and Christianity matters. It is because the love of Christ casts away all fears, makes all things perfect, and it's the calling of every Christian to practice and share Jesus' perfect self-sacrificial love. Though we suffer persecution and indifference and though it seems we're dying out in our native lands in the Middle East—the love of God never fails. Instead, it turns misfortune into joy, suffering into gladness, and desolation into the consolation of the Holy Spirit. Why wouldn't we— whoever or wherever we are in life—want to accept God's invitation to unite our lives to His Divine Life and the Love of Christ?

Blessed are they who are persecuted for the sake of righteousness, for theirs is the kingdom of heaven. Blessed are you when they insult you and persecute you and utter every kind of evil against you [falsely] because of me. Rejoice and be glad, for your reward will be great in heaven. Thus they persecuted the prophets who were before you. (Matt. 5:10-12)

But I say to you, offer no resistance to one who is evil. When someone strikes you on [your] right cheek, turn the other one to him as well. (Matt. 5:39)

"You have heard that it was said, 'You shall love your neighbor and hate your enemy.' But I say to you, love your enemies, and pray for those who persecute you, that you may be children of your heavenly Father, for he makes his sun rise on the bad and the good, and causes rain to fall on the just and the unjust. For if you love those who love you, what recompense will you have? Do not the tax collectors do the same? And if you greet your brothers only, what is unusual about that? Do

not the pagans do the same? So be perfect, just as your heavenly Father is perfect.
(Matt. 5: 43-48)
Stories of the Persecuted

† "How an Iraqi Christian teenager survived two years in the heart of the ISIS 'caliphate'"
  - "My feelings towards ISIS are that I want to completely erase them. But at the same time our religion doesn't promote cruelty. It says 'Whoever hits you on the cheek offer him the other also.'"
  - **https://www.pri.org/stories/2017-01-25/iraqi-christian-teenager-and-his-disabled-mom-barely-escaped-isis**
† "Widow of Palm Sunday Martyr: 'He Asked Me to Wait for Him... But He Never Came Back'"
  - "'I loved him so much,' Sara says. She sees it as a sacrifice for Christ, but not one she has to deal with alone. 'Despite everything, God has put comfort, peace and great grace in my heart.'"
  - **https://www.opendoorsusa.org/christian-persecution/stories/egyptian-widow-of-palm-sunday-martyr-speaks-out/**
† *The 21: A Journey into the Land of Coptic Martyrs* by Marin Mosebach
  - "Life itself, without faith, would have been worthless to them [the Christian martyrs]...That is why I found it repugnant when the Twenty-One were referred to as 'victims of terrorism.'"

Catholicism is rich with symbolism, tradition, and meaning. It's mystical while at the same time the most committed religion to rational explanation. For these reasons, we have a strong foundation and plenty of resources to learn about and share our Faith.

The Bible is a fundamental resource, especially the Gospels and the Torah. The Catechism of the Catholic Church summarizes Catholic beliefs, and C.S. Lewis' *Mere Christianity* is a great introduction to Christianity writ large. In addition, we can recommend Rite of Christian Initiation (RCIA) classes and attend with friends who are interested in learning more about Christianity. It's also a great practice to keep up spiritual reading and to recommend good books we've encountered. I'd also suggest keeping pocket Gospels, Christian pamphlets, or prayer cards on hand and offering them to people who don't yet know Christ. Don't be afraid! Also, check out the brief list of testimonies from Muslims who discovered the truth of Christ in their lives at the end of this chapter. Their stories offer a profound understanding of how to invite Muslims into the Church.

We can also evangelize by remaining faithful to prayer, the Sacraments, and spiritual reflection—which draw us closer to God and provide a deeper understanding of our Faith than intellectual facts. We can spread the Gospel to our Muslim neighbors by sharing what makes our Faith unique, especially our belief in the Love of God. Some people recommend walking directly up to folks and sharing the faith/handing out resources, while others form a relationship first. Pray about how God is calling you to act.

Jesus came to touch hearts, and so let's seek to bring about and pray for a movement of the heart—our hearts and the hearts of all Muslims—towards God. Let us constantly pray for the conversion of the world to the Most Sacred Heart of Jesus. May God bless you!

Testimonies by Former Muslims

†   Daniel Ali: "Preaching Christ Crucified"
  - "I knew that I now had what was needed for my entire nation, indeed for all the Muslims and the unreached world. I had the gospel, and nothing could keep me from sharing it!"
  - **https://chnetwork.org/story/daniel-ali-preaching-christ-crucified/**
†   David Shawkan: "Who is This Man Called Jesus?"

- "Although I was lonely, I never felt alone. There was always Someone, whose identity I did not know, watching over me."
  - **https://chnetwork.org/story/man-called-jesus/**
† Sohrab Ahmari: *From Fire, by Water: My Journey to the Catholic Faith*
- "Life had taught me that our Lord's gift of radical absolution on the Cross was the only thing capable of repairing the brokenness in me and around me."
† Nabeel Qureshi: *Seeking Allah, Finding Jesus*
- "If I had known just how boundless is the love of God…I would have run to Him years sooner with all my might."
- Also check out Nabeel's videos online at **https://www.youtube.com/@MichelleQureshiVlogs/videos**

Other Great Resources to Learn from and Share:

† The Chosen: television series about the life of Jesus (also available in Arabic and multiple other foreign languages)
† The Hallow App
† Dynamic Catholic: for anyone and everyone seeking fulfillment and purpose in life (online and on YouTube)
† Ascension Presents: answers various questions about Catholicism (online and on YouTube)
† The Bible in a Year Podcast (with Fr. Mike Schmitz)

A Humble Invitation

Lastly, I would like to humbly invite you to join me in praying for the conversion of all souls to the light, love, and truth of Christ. Consider praying with your friends and families too—united in the following mission and five simple resolutions.

Mission: To offer prayer and penance for the conversion of all souls to the Sacred Heart of Jesus through the Immaculate Heart of Mary, "especially those who do not believe, do not adore, do not hope, and do not love [the Lord Jesus]," (from the Pardon Prayer, Our Lady of Fatima[11]). Praying for the guidance, joy, and love of God in our hearts, we resolve to:

1. *Pray for the conversion of souls* to the Sacred Heart of Jesus, especially through the Rosary, the Fatima prayer, or offering a Chaplet of Divine Mercy on Fridays
2. *Offer penances as a way of praying always* such as by fasting before receiving the Eucharist on Sundays or abstaining from meat on Fridays to remember Christ's Passion
3. *Grow close to God* in prayer, discernment, spiritual reading, and the Sacraments, which remind us that He is always sustaining, guiding, and lifting us up to Him
4. *Support each other* in bonds of true Christian friendship and help each other unreservedly, even when inconvenient
5. *Evangelize and invite others* to prayer and penance that all might come to love the Lord Jesus.

Our Lady of Fatima, pray for us.

---

[11] Check out *Inside the Light: Understanding the Message of Fatima* by Sr. Angela de Fatima Coelho if you're interested in learning more about Our Lady of Fatima.

Bibliography

Armstrong, Dorsey, 2009. *The Medieval World*. Chantilly: The Teaching Company.

Ehrman, Bart, 1997. *The New Testament: A Historical Introduction To The Early Christian Writings*. 6th ed. Oxford University Press.

Hitti, P. (1970). *Islam: A way of life*. University of Minnesota.

Lapidus, Ira, 2012. *Islamic Societies To The Nineteenth Century*. 1st ed. New York: Cambridge University Press.

Peters, Rudolph, 1995. *Jihad In Classical And Modern Islam*. Princeton: Wiener.